A History of Motor Truck Development

SP-493

Ernest R. Sternberg

Published by:
Society of Automotive Engineers, Inc.
400 Commonwealth Drive, Warrendale, PA 15096
July 1981

ISBN 0-89883-264-0
SAE/SP-81/493
Library of Congress Catalog Card Number: 81-51921
Copyright 1981 Society of Automotive Engineers, Inc.

DEDICATION

To the memory of Wilhelm Sternberg, Ernst M. Sternberg, and William G. Sternberg, who inspired in me an intense interest in motor trucks that continues to this day.

PREFACE

For the past 80 years, motor trucks have served the world by providing one of the most significant means of transportation for practically all of the products we consume and use. Without trucks, our standard of living would be substantially reduced, both due to the lack of general availability of many products and to the higher cost of those products that were available.

During these 80 years, truck development has kept pace with the transportation needs of the world, increasing in capacity, flexibility, performance, and providing a means of efficient transportation at a relatively low cost. Tracing the history of motor truck development during this period of time clearly shows the progress made by motor truck manufacturers and their suppliers with respect to reliability, durability, and overall performance on the road.

Trucks have become more specialized, particularly in the heavier gross weight classes, because of the many industries that depend upon truck transportation. The influence of the varying vehicle size and weight limitations on the development of trucks cannot be over-emphasized.

Today, we stand at a crossroads where it is clearly evident that changes in size and weight limitations are necessary to provide for more efficient truck transportation; efficient not only from the standpoint of moving goods, but also from the standpoint of making the most efficient use of the available fuel supply.

To provide for such improvement, significant changes are required in both size and weight limits, with particular emphasis on the development of more practical length limitations. Provision must be made to haul more cube in many operations due to the low density of general freight.

At the same time, steps must be taken to develop motor trucks conforming to such revised limitations that provide greater fuel efficiency, improved safety, lower operating costs, further improvements in reliability, durability, serviceability, and performance on the road, and provide an improved environment for the driver.

It is fitting that, as a part of the 75th anniversary of the Society of Automotive Engineers, the history of motor trucks should be reviewed. In 1898, the Winton Motor Vehicle Company of Cleveland built the first gasoline powered commercial delivery wagon in the United States, preceding the formation of the SAE by just a few years.

An indicator of the continuing growth in the truck industry is the registration of trucks in the United States, illustrated in Figure 1. Starting in 1905, and with data at ten year intervals through 1975 and then adding 1977, the last year for which total registrations were readily available, a continuous substantial growth is clearly illustrated.

With 1400 registrations in 1905, the growth to almost 2½ million trucks by 1925 is phenomenal; however, in 1945, there were slightly less than 5,000,000 trucks registered, but by 1955 registrations had more than doubled, and by 1977 registrations were almost six times as great as they were in 1945.

It is of interest to review how a number of truck manufacturers entered this business. Autocar, Mack, and White were selected as representative of such manufacturers.

GROWTH OF THE MOTOR TRUCK INDUSTRY
REGISTRATIONS

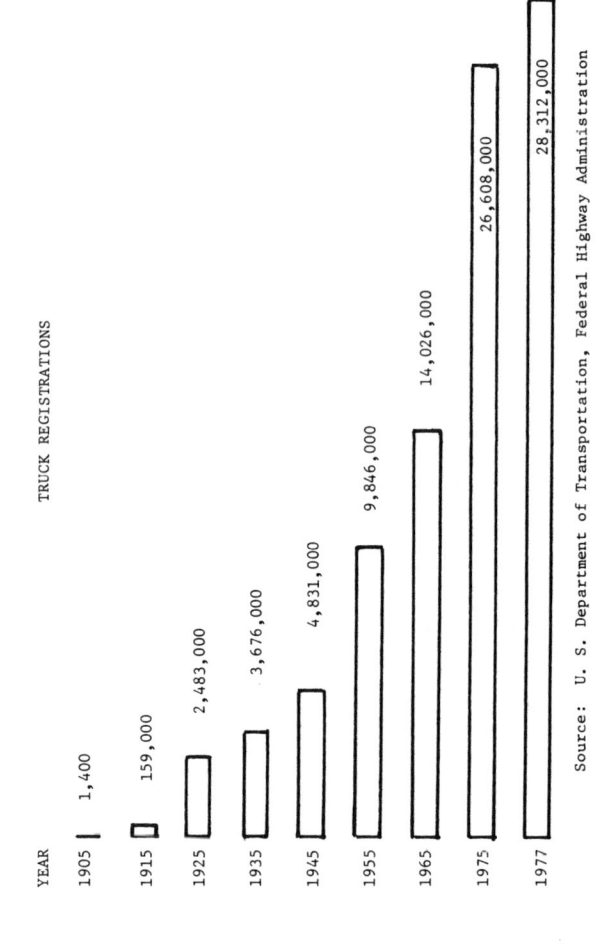

YEAR	TRUCK REGISTRATIONS
1905	1,400
1915	159,000
1925	2,483,000
1935	3,676,000
1945	4,831,000
1955	9,846,000
1965	14,026,000
1975	26,608,000
1977	28,312,000

Source: U. S. Department of Transportation, Federal Highway Administration

Figure 1
Truck Registrations

Autocar had its beginning in 1897 when the Pittsburgh Motor Vehicle Company was formed for the purpose of manufacturing motor vehicles, using a gasoline engine developed by Louis S. Clarke. The engine, a single cylinder, air-cooled type, was first used in a motorized tricycle, produced in 1898.

The second vehicle produced, using a similar engine, but of the two cylinder type, was a light phaeton of the horseless carriage type, using a tiller bar for steering (Figure 2).

Late in 1899, the name of the company was changed to The Autocar Company and operations were moved to Ardmore, Pennsylvania. In 1900, 27 Autocar passenger cars were produced and the following year saw an increase in production to 140 units.

In 1904, Autocar developed the first shaft driven car in America. The Type X Runabout was typical of the Autocars produced in 1904, which were shaft driven, equipped with a 10 horsepower, two cylinder engine, a 3-speed transmission and left hand drive with a steering lever arrangement. Interestingly enough, at that time, there was so much resistance to the left hand drive that it was necessary to revert back to right hand drive on subsequent models, including the early Autocar trucks.

In 1907, Autocar produced its first truck, a 1½-2 ton model with the engine located under the seat. With minor changes, this type of truck went into production in 1908. A single searchlight was mounted on the forward panel and on the vehicle illustrated in Figure 3 (produced in 1910), two oil lamps were mounted at the front of the body. Note the rolled-up front and side covers for the body. Cargo protection was considered to be more important than protection for the driver who was fully exposed to the weather.

By 1910, Autocar had discontinued the manufacture of passenger cars and concentrated its production efforts on the 1½ ton truck of the engine under the seat type, which was its sole product until 1919. Over 30,000 such vehicles

Figure 2

Autocar No. 2 – Phaeton (1898) *(Photograph furnished through the courtesy of the White Motor Corporation)*

Figure 3
Autocar 1½-2 Ton Engine Under the Seat Truck (1910)
(Photograph furnished through the courtesy of the
White Motor Corporation)

were produced.

Five Mack brothers were instrumental in forming Mack trucks.[1] One of the brothers started working for a Brooklyn, New York carriage and wagon manufacturer in 1889. A second brother went to work for the firm in 1890. In 1893, the two brothers took over the factory, with a third brother joining them in 1894. Since the brothers preferred to build wagons, the carriage business was gradually phased out.

There were many horse drawn sightseeing stages used in the Brooklyn area. Interest was expressed in a gasoline powered bus by one of the stage operators. The Mack brothers built a bus to fill this requirement. They originally used a 4 cylinder opposed engine purchased from an engine manufacturer but within a year, had changed the engine to a 4 cylinder vertical engine of their own manufacture.

The name Manhattan was given to the buses and by 1904 their buses had grown in size. In 1905, the Mack brothers moved to Allentown, Pennsylvania where a fourth brother joined the firm and they continued to build sightseeing buses. They also received orders for hotel buses and a combination express and passenger vehicle.

In addition, they contemplated the construction of motor trucks during 1904, but pilot model production did not take place until 1905. Several trucks (which also carried the name Manhattan) were finished and thoroughly tested during that year. The vehicles consisted of two delivery trucks with a nominal 1½-2 ton capacity and a 5 ton truck with the driver's seat over the engine.

The basic Mack engine was developed in 1905 and was produced with relatively few changes until about 1915. This engine was of the 4 cylinder type with a 5½" bore and 6" stroke and developed 50 horsepower at 1000 r.p.m.

---

[1]The data on Mack trucks are based on the book, MACK, A Living Legend of the Highway, by John B. Montville, Copyright 1979, by John B. Montville and Aztex Corporation, and published by Aztex Corporation, P.O. Box 50046, Tucson, AZ 85703.

The same basic engines and transmissions were used in the 2,3,4, and 5 ton Manhattan trucks.

In the 1908-1909 period, a line of engine-in-front (conventional) models up to 5 ton capacity, paralleling the engine under the seat models, was developed.

In 1909, Mack introduced a new line of trucks, rated at 1, 1½, and 2 ton capacity and equipped with a smaller engine rated at 32 horsepower. These smaller trucks were designated as the Junior Line while trucks of 3 ton capacity and over were designated as the Senior Line.

The fifth brother joined the firm in 1910. Shortly thereafter, the Manhattan name was dropped and all trucks leaving the Allentown plant carried the name 'Mack'.

The manufacture of White trucks dates back to 1859 when the White Sewing Machine Company was started in Cleveland to manufacture sewing machines. In 1899, Rollin White, the son of the founder, invented an automotive type flash boiler. The first steamer, a passenger car, was completed in 1900.

This car was followed by the production of a light steam delivery truck delivered early in 1901 to the Denver Dry Goods Company of Denver, Colorado (Figure 4). There was a strong resemblance to the passenger car, including tires, wire wheels, steering tiller, and the general front end configuration.

By late 1901, White was building up to three cars per week and work was started on a 5 ton steam truck which was delivered in 1902. The boiler was located next to the driver.

White continued to build steam powered passenger cars for a number of years. 1500 vehicles were produced in 1906, over twice as many as produced by any other manufacturer.

During 1906, White produced an 18 horsepower steam ambulance of conventional design for the U.S. Government. In 1909, White produced its first gasoline powered car, and in 1910, its first gasoline powered truck, a 3 ton con-

Figure 4
First White Steam Delivery Truck (1901) (Photograph furnished through the courtesy of the White Motor Corporation)

Figure 5
White 3 Ton Gasoline Powered Truck (1910) (Photograph furnished through the courtesy of the White Motor Corporation)

ventional model with solid tires mounted on metal wheels, illustrated in Figure 5. White discontinued the manufacture of passenger cars in 1918 to concentrate on the manufacture of trucks.

In tracing the history of the development of motor trucks, it was concluded that a viable approach was to separate truck developments into ten year increments beginning with 1900-1910 and provide a brief description of the major characteristics of trucks for that period, together with descriptions of representative trucks.

The characteristics are somewhat general and do not necessarily apply to all trucks produced during a specific period.

1900-1910

In the 1900-1910 period, motor trucks were in their infancy. Practically all trucking took place within the cities. There was no such thing as inter-city trucking due to the fact that the roads between cities were completely inadequate. Early configurations were quite similar to wagons with the engines located under the seat or under the floor.

Among the typical characteristics of trucks produced in that period were:
- Gasoline, steam and electrical power available.
- Right hand drive.
- Engine usually located under an open seat; 2 or 4 cylinders; low horsepower, low r.p.m.
- Magneto ignition on gasoline engines.
- Oil or acetylene headlamps.
- Solid tires except on light delivery vehicles.
- Final drive by chains and sprockets.
- Transmissions usually amidship mounted.
- Mechanical band type brakes commonly used.
- Wood spoke wheels.
- Maximum speeds 8-12 m.p.h. (except light delivery trucks).

• Capacity rating given in terms of tons of nominal payload.

In addition to the early Autocar, Mack, and White trucks discussed above, the following were typical vehicles of the 1900-1910 period:

1½ Ton Light Delivery Truck — A truck, used to deliver candy, was of the engine under the seat type with right hand drive, wood spoke wheels, solid tires, and chain drive. A horn was mounted on the dash with the bulb located under the steering wheel. An open seat with a projection from the body over the driver's head was provided, but no windshield.

5 Ton Chain Drive Dump Truck — This truck (Figure 6) was of the engine under the seat type with an open seat. No windshield or other protective devices were provided for the driver. A mechanical hoist was operated manually by means of a crank (before the days of the hydraulic hoist installations). The vehicle was equipped with wood spoke wheels, solid tires, right hand drive, with the final drive provided by means of chains and sprockets.

White ¾ Ton Delivery Truck — Delivery trucks of conventional design were produced in 1910. The truck was equipped with right hand drive. Due to its light weight, pneumatic tires were used. The body extended over the driver's seat to provide some protection for the driver.

1911-1920

In the 1911-1920 period, limited usage of trucks between cities began to take place as roads were improved to a certain extent. Many new uses of trucks were developed. The general truck characteristics and developments for this period include:

• Engine under the seat design predominant through 1914-1915; largely changed to conventional design by 1915.

• Gasoline engines used in most trucks, but there was some continued use of electric and gas-electric power.

Figure 6
5 Ton Chain Drive Dump Truck (1909)

- 4 cylinder engines substantially outnumber the 2 cylinder type; the horsepower range was 30-50; engine speeds ranged from 950-1500 r.p.m.
- Most trucks still used chains for final drive but there was increasing usage of bevel, worm and double reduction gear drive rear axles.
- Trucks were often equipped with a roof extended over the driver and passenger seats; a few were equipped with windshields.
- Right hand drive largely used through 1914; a rapid change to left hand drive thereafter.
- Some limited usage of semi-trailers and full trailers.
- Magneto ignition.
- Introduction of electric headlamps.
- 3- and 4-speed transmissions most popular; some usage of unit power plant construction (transmission mounted in unit with the engine).
- Some usage of high pressure pneumatic tires on 1½-2 ton trucks.
- Wood spoke wheels most popular; some use of steel spoke wheels.
- Maximum speeds 10-15 m.p.h. with solid tires; up to 35 m.p.h. with pneumatic tires.

Typical of the trucks produced during the 1911-1920 time period are the following:

2 Ton Truck — This truck was produced in 1912 and is of the engine under the seat type with right hand drive. High pressure pneumatic tires were installed on the front axle with solid tires on the rear axle. Final drive is by means of chains and sprockets. Headlamps are of the acetylene type.

3 Ton Gear Drive Truck Chassis — This truck chassis was produced in early 1915 (Figure 7). It is of the conventional design with the engine mounted in front of the fire wall. It has right hand drive and is equipped with a partial cab, but without a windshield or doors. The rear axle is of the worm gear drive type; wood spoke wheels were supplied.

Figure 7
3 Ton Conventional Gear Drive Chassis (1915)

White 1½-2 Ton Gasoline Delivery Truck — Typical of vehicles produced in 1915, this truck is of conventional design and is equipped with left hand drive, wood spoke wheels, and solid tires (Figure 8). A partial cab was supplied with a windshield of the curtain type which could be rolled up under the extension over the driver's seat.

5 Ton Tractor with Semi-Trailer — Produced late in 1915 or early 1916, this 5 ton conventional truck was set up as a tractor for use with a large bottom dump semi-trailer of the wagon type. The trailer was equipped with wood spoke wheels with flat steel tires.

Mack AC Prototype — The prototype of the famous Mack model AC, produced in 3½, 5½, and 7½ ton capacities, was built in 1915 and equipped with a 74 horsepower, 4 cylinder engine. This model, with its sloping hood and radiator located to the rear of the engine, was responsible for the name 'Bulldog' being applied to Mack trucks and was in production for more than twenty years.

Tractor with Semi-Trailer — In 1916, a Mack heavy-duty model AC tractor was used to haul milk in the New York City area. The cab was equipped with half doors and with rolled-up curtains at the front and sides for use under poor weather conditions. The tractor was equipped with solid tires mounted on wood spoke wheels, but the trailer was fitted with large diameter steel tired wagon wheels.

White 5 Ton Truck with Full Trailer — This illustration (Figure 9) is of an early truck and full trailer combination produced in 1918. The truck is of the chain drive type with the body extending over the driver's seat. Solid tires were provided on both the truck and the trailer.

Mack Model AB with Open Express Body — First introduced in 1914, the Mack model AB was equipped with a 4 cylinder engine developing a little over 30 horsepower and a 3-speed transmission bolted directly to the flywheel housing. While worm gear drive axles were first offered, chain drive was also offered shortly thereafter. This model was originally built in 1, 1½ and 2 ton capacity.

Figure 8
White 1½-2 Ton Gasoline Delivery Truck (1915)
(Photograph furnished through the courtesy of the White Motor Corporation)

Figure 9
White 5 Ton Truck with Full Trailer (1918) (Photograph furnished through the courtesy of the White Motor Corporation)

Logging Truck and Trailer — A White logging truck produced in 1916, was of the chain drive type and equipped with left hand drive. The most interesting feature was the use of steel tires and integral wheels on both the truck and the trailer, required due to the fact that this unit operated on bull-dozed roads in an area with considerable rainfall.

White Double Reduction Rear Axle — In 1918, White developed an internal gear drive axle with the first reduction through a set of bevel gears at the differential assembly located at the center of the axle (Figure 10). The second reduction took place at the outer ends of the axle with the drive from a gear mounted at the outer end of each axle shaft, meshing with a single idler gear which in turn drove the internal gear.

Class B Military Truck — This illustration (Figure 11) shows a group of the standardized U.S. Army Class B military trucks of 3½ ton capacity, ready to be driven away from a truck factory. These trucks were built to a standardized design by a number of truck manufacturers. The military services also purchased lighter and heavier trucks from various manufacturers.

Goodyear Wingfoot Highway Express — In 1920, Goodyear operated a fleet of trucks equipped with pneumatic tires in long haul operations, such as from Akron to Boston and return. The intent was to prove the reliability of high pressure pneumatic tires. Since single rear tires were used, the rear tires were much larger than the front tires.

1921-1930

There was considerable development and expanded usage of trucks during the 1921-1930 time period. Among the general truck characteristics applicable to such vehicles were the following:
- Almost entirely conventional design.
- Left hand drive.

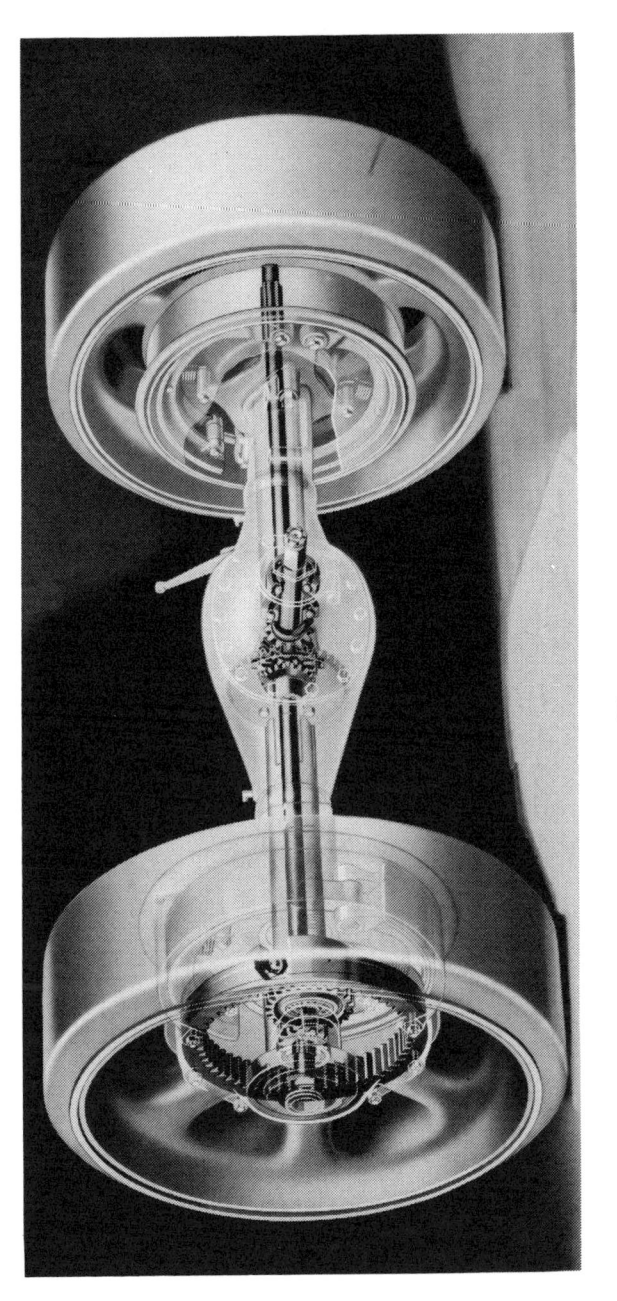

Figure 10
*White Double Reduction Gear Drive Axle (1918)
(Photograph furnished through the courtesy of the
White Motor Corporation)*

Figure 11
Class B 3½ Ton Standardized Military Truck (1918)

- Practically all gasoline powered; electric trucks largely phased out by 1928.
- 4 cylinder engines used exclusively during the early part of the period; 6 cylinder engines introduced in the latter part.
- 4 cylinder engines range in horsepower from 40-70; r.p.m. range 1000-1500. 6 cylinder engines range from 50-100 horsepower; r.p.m. range 1800-2500.
- Distributor ignition on lighter units; magneto ignition on heavier units.
- Electric starting available on most trucks.
- Final drive — worm drive was the most popular but there was more usage of bevel gear drive on the lighter units.
- Increasing use of pneumatic tires; solid tires still predominate on heavier units.
- 4 wheel hydraulic brakes introduced; increasing usage of vacuum booster brakes and some usage of early air brake systems.
- Increased use of semi-trailers and full trailers.
- Most trucks equipped with a cab having a windshield and half doors with curtains; early usage of fully enclosed cabs; introduction of sleeper cabs.
- 3- to 7-speed transmissions used; most mounted in unit with the engine; introduction of 3-speed auxiliary transmissions.
- 3 axle trucks with single driving axles and with tandem driving axles introduced.
- Early usage of lightweight aluminum alloy parts.
- Concrete mixer units introduced.
- Maximum speeds 20-30 m.p.h. on solid tires; 30-45 m.p.h. on pneumatic tires.

Typical of the vehicles and improvements incorporated in vehicles during the 1921-1930 time period were the following:

3½ **Ton Truck with Van Type Body** — Produced in 1922, this truck (Figure 12) illustrates the early use of a

Figure 12
3½ Ton Truck with Van Type Body (1922)

fully enclosed cab. The rear axle was of the worm gear drive type. Solid tires mounted on steel spoke wheels were supplied.

Mack AC in Drayage Service — A 1928 Mack model AC, used in drayage service along the New York waterfront, employed a cab fitted with a windshield and half doors. Solid rubber tires mounted on cast steel wheels were supplied. Final drive was by means of chains and sprockets.

White 5 Ton Tractor with Triples Trailers — Intended for gasoline transport, this illustration (Figure 13) shows the early use of multiple trailers. Prior to 1930, there were few limits on overall lengths of vehicles or combinations, nor were there many restrictions on the number of units that could be used in combinations. The tractor was equipped with a double reduction rear axle and high pressure single pneumatic tires, with a much larger size being used on the rear axle. Solid tires were furnished on the three trailers.

5 Ton Long Wheelbase Truck with Full Trailer — A typical 3 axle West Coast truck and 3 axle full trailer combination manufactured in 1926 consisted of a 5 ton truck equipped with a third axle, utilizing dual solid tires on the double reduction drive axle and single solid tires on the attachment axle. At that time, most attachment axles were installed locally rather than at the truck manufacturer's plant.

Early 6 Cylinder Gasoline Engine Installation — This illustration (Figure 14) shows the installation of a relatively large displacement 6 cylinder engine produced in 1928. The engine had a piston displacement of approximately 550 cubic inches and developed 95 horsepower at 1800 r.p.m. The engine was equipped with magneto ignition and had its cylinders cast in blocks of two and bolted to the crankcase assembly.

Heavy Duty Tandem Rear Driving Axle — Most tandem axles which were installed in this time period were of

Figure 13
White 5 Ton Tractor with Triples Trailers (1927)
(Photograph furnished through the courtesy of the White Motor Corporation)

Figure 14
Early 6 Cylinder Gasoline Engine Installation (1928)

the dual worm gear type without an inter-axle differential. The suspension was of the walking beam type with relatively complicated linkage to maintain axle alignment and to provide for articulation.

Aluminum Tandem Rear Axle Assembly — Fageol, a West Coast truck manufacturer, offered an aluminum tandem rear axle assembly in 1929. It was of the dual worm gear drive type and had aluminum axle housings, differential carrier housings, brake shoes, hubs, and suspension parts, resulting in a substantial reduction in weight.

Aluminum Frame Assembly — The Fageol truck was also offered with a frame assembly consisting of deep section aluminum side rails, cross-members, and frame brackets, thereby providing an exceptionally lightweight truck (Figure 15).

Early Concrete Mixer Installation — Early concrete hauling trucks were equipped with an open agitator type body for keeping the concrete relatively fluid during delivery to the job site. The mixed concrete was poured into the body and then agitated by blades driven by a separate engine or through a power take-off, depending upon the type of mixer.

Early Autocar Conventional Trucks — Because of the acceptance of its engine under the seat models, Autocar did not produce any trucks of conventional design until late in 1926. Early models were equipped with a cab which did not incorporate a windshield or doors as standard equipment.

1931-1940

The 1931-1940 time period included the depression years. Surprisingly enough, there were a substantial number of new developments made during this period. Size and weight restrictions became of considerable importance and had an important influence on truck design.

Among the truck characteristics of interest during this

Figure 15
Fageol Aluminum Frame Assembly (1929)

period were the following:
- While most trucks were of conventional design, demand for cab over engine trucks began to develop again due to restrictive length limitations imposed by a number of states.
- Development of the forward tilting cab on cab over engine trucks substantially improved engine accessibility for servicing purposes.
- Gasoline engines predominate; practically all 6 cylinder engines with some V8s (especially in smaller sizes). 60-150 horsepower range; 1800-2500 r.p.m. (higher on small V8s).
- Diesel engines introduced in 1931; somewhat limited usage but substantial reduction in fuel costs of interest to operators. 4 cylinder 85 horsepower and 6 cylinder 125 horsepower engines originally made available.
- Worm gear drive single rear axles phased out and replaced with spiral bevel and double reduction gear drive axles. Worm drive tandem axles continue in use.
- Trend to more 3 axle trucks.
- Considerable use of third axle conversions on light trucks to haul heavier payloads.
- Increasing use of 3-speed auxiliary transmissions with four- or five-speed unit transmissions.
- Vacuum booster actuated hydraulic brakes or air brakes used on practically all heavy trucks.
- Low pressure balloon tires phased in and by 1934 used on practically all heavy trucks.
- Wheels — steel spoke and steel disc.
- Increasing use of lightweight aluminum construction.
- Most trucks equipped with fully enclosed cabs; many cabs of all steel construction. Considerably more usage of sleeper cabs as lengths of haul increased.
- Speeds up to 50 m.p.h. common.
- Trucks rated by gross vehicle weight (sum of chassis, body, and payload weights) in lieu of nominal payload (tonnage) ratings.

Typical vehicles and product improvements incorporated in vehicles during the 1931-1940 time period include:

Gasoline Delivery Truck — Produced in the early 1930s, this White truck featured clean, functional lines (Figure 16). It was equipped with a fully enclosed cab, gear driven rear axle, steel spoke wheels, demountable rims, and pneumatic tires with dual tires on the rear axle.

Mack Short-Coupled Truck — Introduced in 1933, the Mack C series short-coupled trucks had the radiator and a short hood projecting about 2 feet in front of the cab, which was fixed in place. The model CH was rated at 3-5 ton capacity and intended for use in congested city areas.

Early Installation of Diesel Engine — This diesel engine installation, made in 1931, was one of the first original equipment installations of diesel engines made in a conventional truck at a truck manufacturer's plant (Figure 17). The engine was the Cummins model H6 with a piston displacement of 672 cubic inches and developed 125 horsepower at 1800 r.p.m. Note the size of the fuel pump at the lower center of the engine.

Gasoline Tanker Truck — The 1934 Mack BQ three axle truck was equipped with a 128 horsepower gasoline engine and often used in gasoline transport service.

Heavy-Duty Dual Chain Drive Dump Truck — Produced in 1935, this heavy duty dual chain drive dump truck (Figure 18) was designed to carry 18 tons of lead ore at altitudes up to 14,000 feet in the Andes Mountains in Chile. Because of the potential power loss of 35-40% at such high altitudes, it was necessary to provide a supercharger to retain sea level power at 14,000 feet.

Supercharger Installation — The supercharger of the Rootes blower type was installed in 1935, a number of years before Cummins offered supercharged engines (Figure 19). The engine was of the Cummins H6 type to which the supercharger was added. The installation was successful as evidenced by the fact that all future purchases made by this operator were tractor semi-trailer combinations

Figure 16
White Gasoline Delivery Truck (1932) (Photograph furnished through the courtesy of the White Motor Corporation)

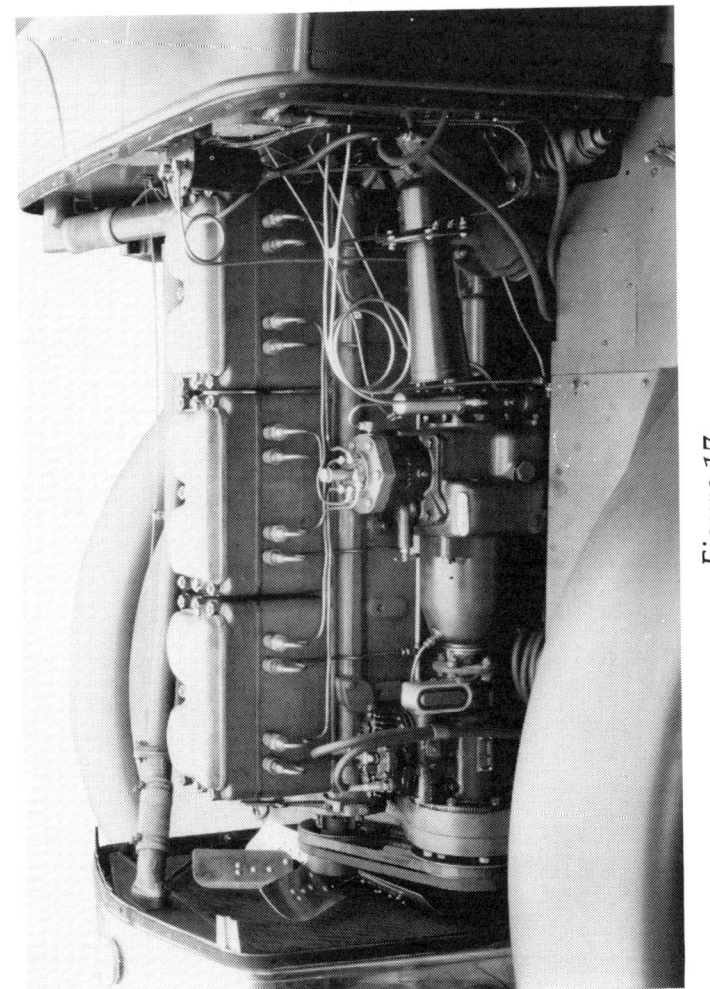

Figure 17
Early Diesel Engine Installation (1931)

Figure 18
Heavy-Duty Dump Truck with Supercharged Diesel Engine (1935)

Figure 19
Supercharger Installation on Diesel Engine (1935)

equipped with side dump bodies to haul 25-30 ton payloads, using the same engine and supercharger installation.

Cab Over Engine Tractor with Rearward Tilting Cab — With the increasing stringency of overall length limits, the need for cab over engine trucks and tractors substantially increased. A major problem that developed with the fixed cabs used at that time was poor accessibility to the engine compartment for servicing. To provide improved accessibility over the fixed cab construction, one approach used was to tilt the upper rear part of this cab, including the doors, to the rear. While this construction was a substantial improvement over the fixed cab, it still did not provide adequate accessibility.

Cab Over Engine Truck with 12 Cylinder Pancake Engine — Another effort to provide improved engine accessibility in cab over engine trucks resulted in the use of a 12 cylinder pancake engine mounted on a sub-frame with the radiator, clutch, and transmission assembly sliding out as a single unit (Figure 20). The cab was fixed in place but the grill at the front of the cab was readily removable.

Slide-Out Engine Assembly Installation — Figure 21 shows the engine installation after it had slid forward on the sub-frame and been removed from the truck for servicing.

Cab Over Engine Lightweight Tractor with Tank Type Semi-Trailer — Produced in 1935, a milestone vehicle was of the short wheelbase cab over engine type designed to haul 3800 gallons of gasoline within 38,000 pounds gross combination weight (Figure 22). This truck was equipped with an aluminum cab, frame rails, crossmembers, brackets, fuel tank, and battery box. A 100 horsepower 6 cylinder Waukesha diesel engine was used.

While the substantial use of aluminum and lightweight construction in this tractor was important, its most outstanding feature was the fact that it had the first practical forward tilting cab installation in which the complete cab assembly with most controls, pedals, steering column, and

Figure 20
White Cab Over Engine Truck with 12 Cylinder Pancake Engine (1936)(Photograph furnished through the courtesy of the White Motor Corporation)

Figure 21
12 Cylinder Pancake Engine with Slide-Out Provisions (1936) (Photograph furnished through the courtesy of the White Motor Corporation)

Figure 22
First Practical Forward Tilting Cab Installation
(1935)

37

fenders tilted forward to provide excellent accessibility to the engine. For the first time, cab over engine trucks really became practical from a servicing and maintenance point of view. Now all U. S. and most European and Japanese trucks of the cab over engine type are equipped with a forward tilting cab.

Cab Over Engine Sleeper Cab Tractor with Doubles Trailers — Due to the restrictive length limits that applied in 1936, an early use of doubles trailers made it necessary to locate the sleeper compartment above the driver's compartment instead of to the rear. The cab was constructed of aluminum and was of the forward tilting type.

1½ Ton Truck with Third Axle Installation — During the depression years, there was substantial interest in building up light trucks into heavier capacity units by adding third axle attachments (Figure 23). A typical third axle installation included frame reinforcements, additional crossmembers, a complete trailing axle with brakes, hubs and drums, suspension parts, and four additional tires and wheels. A vehicle of this type was used to haul payloads up to 10 tons. While the life of some components, such as the engine, under such conditions was relatively short, their low replacement cost had considerable appeal.

Mack FJ Concrete Mixer Truck — In 1939, Mack produced their model FJ equipped with a 131 horsepower Mack-Lanova diesel engine and with chain drive. It was often used in concrete mixer service. For construction use, many operators continued to favor cabs with half doors.

Streamline Tractor — Towards the end of this time period, considerable interest developed in the styling and streamlining of trucks and tractors. White tractors for example, were styled by a well-known industrial designer.

1941-1950

The 1941-1950 time period included World War II and therefore it is necessary to divide it into 2 five-year

Figure 23
Ford Truck with Third Axle Installation (1934)

periods since practically no new commercial truck development took place between 1941 and 1945.

During this time period, the truck manufacturing industry devoted its facilities to the manufacture of trucks and other war products for the U. S. Armed Services and its allies.

Trucks produced for the military services in 1941-1945 included:

Half-Track Vehicles — Half-track vehicles were equipped with a conventional front steering axle but with crawler tracks at the rear (Figure 24). Various versions of half-track vehicles were produced. Most of these units were built by White, Autocar, and Diamond T.

Aircraft Recovery Trucks — Aircraft recovery trucks were used by the U. S. Navy Bureau of Aeronautics to recover disabled aircraft operating from land bases. These trucks were equipped with 3 driving axles and featured a large crane mounted in back of the cab.

Aircraft Crash Trucks — 6 X 6 fire crash trucks were used by the U. S. Army Air Corps to spray carbon dioxide foam on crashed and/or burning aircraft (Figure 25).

British Army Tank Transporter — The Mack NR-4 six wheeler was developed as a tank transporter for the British Army for use in the North African Campaign. A heat shield was furnished on the roof of the cab. Right hand drive was required.

Commercial truck production was resumed late in 1944 on a limited basis under priorities granted by the War Production Board. The time required to phase out military contracts and to convert to civilian production resulted in relatively low production in 1945. Truck production in 1946 was approximately 50% higher than in 1945 and in 1947 almost double that of 1945.

Typical of the truck characteristics and product improvements incorporated in trucks during 1946-1950 were the following:

- Conventional trucks still predominate but a substan-

Figure 24
Autocar Half-Track (1942-1945) (Photograph furnished through the courtesy of the White Motor Corporation)

Figure 25
Army Air Corps Fire Crash Truck (1943)

tial increase in the use of cab over engine tractors with sleeper cabs was brought about by overall length restrictions and the longer hauls.
- First high production forward tilting cab over engine trucks introduced.
- Introduction of high speed, high performance gasoline engines.
- Additional diesel engine availability results in increasing use of diesel engines in long haul operations. 100-200 horsepower; 1800-2200 r.p.m.
- Alternators being used in limited quantities in lieu of generators.
- Greater use of power steering for heavy front axle loadings.

Typical of production during the 1946-1950 time frame were the following:

High Production Truck with Forward Tilting Cab — The previous cab over engine trucks equipped with a forward tilting cab had been produced in relatively low volume. The White 3000 series were the first high production cab over engine trucks available with forward tilting cabs (Figure 26). The cab was tilted by means of an electrically actuated tilting device. This basic series was in production from 1949-1967.

High Performance Gasoline Engines — Gasoline engines during this period were substantially improved through the use of new designs to provide higher operating speeds and higher horsepower per cubic inch of piston displacement (Figure 27). They incorporated premium long life features such as stellite faced valves and valve seat inserts, sodium cooled valves, electrically hardened crankshafts, and hydraulic valve lifters.

1951-1960

During the 1951-1960 time period, truck use expanded substantially. In addition, trucks were becoming more

Figure 26
White 3000 Series Truck with Tilt Cab (1949)
(Photograph furnished through the courtesy of the White Motor Corporation)

Figure 27
White Mustang High Speed Gasoline Engine (1947)
(Photograph furnished through the courtesy of the White Motor Corporation)

sophisticated and were equipped with many more optional items than had formerly been specified.

In the 1951-1960 period, truck characteristics of interest were the following:

- Good demand continued to exist for both conventional and cab over engine trucks. Short nose conventional tractors with a 90-92" bumper to back of cab dimension were made available to permit hauling 40 foot semi-trailers within 50 foot overall length.
- Diamond T and International introduced counterbalanced spring tilt cabs on cab over engine trucks.
- Diesel engine penetration in heavy trucks increased substantially. The first turbo-charged diesel engines were placed in production. Horsepower range 125-335; 1800-2500 r.p.m.
- Clutches were practically all single and two plate types.
- Range shift transmissions with single lever control introduced.
- Steering pusher axle installations with single tires on the pusher axle and dual tires on drive axle introduced.
- Most highway tractors are of the 3 axle type because of changes in state weight laws.
- Increasing use of lightweight materials, such as aluminum and fiberglass.
- Tubeless tires with drop center one piece rims available for use on heavy trucks.
- Wide base flotation tires introduced to permit using single tires on rear axles.
- Lightweight spiral bevel and hypoid gear drive tandem rear axles introduced. Because of lower maintenance costs and lighter weight, they quickly became popular and largely replaced the worm gear drive tandem axles previously used in highway operations.
- First trucks equipped with a reinforced fiberglass cab introduced.
- 3 axle tractors hauling 2 forty foot trailers and

equipped with 335 horsepower diesel engines successfully tested on the New York Thruway.

Typical of the vehicles produced during this period are the following:

2 Axle Tractor with Bottom Dump Doubles Trailers — A typical combination used during this period consisted of a 2 axle long hood diesel powered conventional tractor with bottom dump doubles trailers used to haul sugar in a West Coast operation.

3 Axle Lightweight Tractor — Another typical West Coast combination was the Mack LTLSW 3 axle lightweight tractor hauling a large bulk cement semi-trailer. A long tractor wheelbase was supplied to permit hauling the maximum gross weight under Bridge Formula requirements.

Mack Model B61ST 3 Axle Tractor — Introduced in the mid-1950s, the Mack model B61ST tractor had frame rails that were wider at the front to permit the installation of larger engines. This tractor was normally equipped with a vertical muffler installation.

Short Nose Conventional Tractor — To haul a 40 foot semi-trailer within an overall length of 50 feet, a demand developed for conventional tractors with a dimension from the front bumper to the back of the cab of 90-92". In this design, the engine projects partially into the cab but a short hood is retained. Illustrated is an early version of the White 9000 series short nose conventional tractor (Figure 28).

Cab Over Engine Truck with Full Trailer — Typical of truck and full trailer combinations in use was the Freightliner 3 axle cab over engine truck equipped with a non-sleeper cab and set up for use with a full trailer and with tanks mounted on both the truck and the trailer. In order to provide maximum payload in a bulk haul operation, the truck was equipped with an aluminum cab, crossmembers, frame brackets, bumper, fuel tanks, and battery box.

Truck with Counter-Balanced Spring Tilt Cab — Diamond Reo and International Harvester produced cab

Figure 28
White 9000 Series Short Nose Conventional Tractor (1958) (Photograph furnished through the courtesy of the White Motor Corporation)

over engine trucks with the cab of the forward tilting type, counter-balanced around the neutral point through the installation of coil springs depressed when the cab is in its normal driving position. The springs exert an upward force so that relatively little manual effort was required to tilt the cab forward and return it to its normal position.

Tractor with Reinforced Fiberglass Cab — The White 5000 series were the first tractors equipped with a reinforced fiberglass cab. Introduced in 1959, this series was made available with a 50" dimension from bumper to back of cab with a non-sleeper cab. Both short and long sleeper cabs were also available.

One of the tractors used to haul two forty foot trailers on the New York Thruway was this White 5000 series turnpike tractor (Figure 29). The overall combination length was 98 feet. These tractors are required to maintain a minimum speed of 20 m.p.h. on a 3% grade. With the maximum gross weight of 127,400 pounds, an engine developing 335 gross horsepower was required. Various turnpikes and thruways continue to permit the use of such combinations which have an excellent safety record.

Wide Base Flotation Tires — Wide base flotation tires were developed for use as single tire installations on front and rear axles loaded to maximum permissible axle weights. The tires are of the tubeless type and are used with a one piece drop center rim. An important advantage was the large weight saving when replacing dual rear tires. These tires have met with good acceptance for use on heavily loaded front axles in operations involving both on and off highway operations but only limited acceptance for use on rear axles.

3 Axle Oil Field Truck — Figure 30 illustrates the severity of skid loading in oil field operations. The truck is equipped with winches mounted in back of the cab and is engaged in sliding a heavy draw works up a ramp onto the back of the truck. With the weight concentrated at a point back of the center line between the two rear axles, the front

Figure 29
White 5000 Series Turnpike Tractor (1959) (Photograph furnished through the courtesy of the White Motor Corporation)

Figure 30
Heavy-Duty Oil Field Truck (1952)

end of the truck is lifted completely off the ground. As the draw works is pulled forward, the front end drops down to its normal position.

Mack D Series with Verti-Lift Cab — In 1955, Mack introduced their D series cab over engine trucks with a cab that raised vertically by either the standard manual or the optional hydraulic lifting mechanism to provide accessibility to the engine for servicing.

Mack H Series Cab Over Engine Tractor — Mack introduced a modified version of their H series cab over engine tractors in 1954. The design modification lowered the overall height of the cab, which was of the forward tilting type, by one foot.

1961-1970

Truck characteristics of interest during the 1961-1970 time period are as follows:
- No substantial changes in configurations or in dimensions.
- Greater use of diesel engines including shorter haul operations. Horsepower requirements continue to increase. Up to 450 horsepower used in limited quantities. Much greater use of turbo-charged engines.
- Mack Maxidyne engine, with relatively constant horsepower and 50% torque rise made available and quickly gains operator and drive acceptance.
- Testing of gas turbines in trucks underway. Fuel economy not as good as on diesel engines.
- Higher capacity single reduction tandem axles made available for use with higher horsepower engines.
- Doubles trailers increase in popularity due to higher cube available for low density freight operations.
- Wedge type disc brakes with automatic adjustment produced by several manufacturers.
- Many conventional trucks equipped with tilting integral hood and fender assembly for improved engine

accessibility.
- Air suspension seats becoming popular.
- Initial Federal Safety Standards effective after December 1968; others effective after December 1969.
- First emission standards applicable to gasoline engines.
- Substantial increase in requirements for custom engineering to meet individual customer requirements.
- Air ride suspensions for single and tandem rear axles made available by several manufacturers.
- Spring actuated parking brakes used almost exclusively on heavy trucks equipped with air brakes.

Among the vehicles illustrating units of the type produced during 1961-1970 are the following:

2 Axle Tractor with Doubles Trailers — The use of doubles trailers became of increasing importance due to the fact that general freight has an average density of 12 pounds per cubic foot. In such operations, the maximum gross combination weight that can be hauled is largely dependent upon the cubical contents of the trailers. Two 27 foot trailers can be hauled within an overall length of 65 feet and provide substantially greater cubical contents than available in a single 45 foot semi-trailer. The illustration (Figure 31) shows a typical doubles combination with a non-sleeper cab equipped tractor.

Half Cab Mixer Truck — A one man cab (termed a half cab) mounted alongside the engine is used on this Autocar mixer truck (Figure 32) to provide better visibility, a shorter wheelbase, and greater maneuverability on the job site. The engine is set back in the frame to make provision for a front end power take-off drive and for mounting the hydraulic pump back of the front bumper.

Long BBC 3 Axle Tractor with Sleeper Box — While cab over engine tractors are usually available with sleeper berths integral with the cab assembly, most conventional tractors requiring a sleeper berth utilize a separate sleeper box mounted directly to the rear of the non-sleeper cab and

Figure 31
White 7400 Series Tractor with Doubles Trailers (1963) (Photograph furnished through the courtesy of the White Motor Corporation)

Figure 32
Autocar Half Cab Mixer Truck (1967) (Photograph furnished through the courtesy of the White Motor Corporation)

connected by means of a relatively large opening.

Cab Over Engine Tractor with Double Width Sleeper Berth — Freightliner and several other manufacturers made available cab over engine tractors with a sleeper cab having a double width berth (approximately 54" wide). The demand for such units has increased due to the number of man and wife driving teams (sometimes with one or two children) who travel together at least part of the year.

1971-1980

Truck characteristics for 1971-1980 and some of the developments which took place during that time period are as follows:

- The most popular highway tractor configurations are the short nose conventional design and the sleeper cab equipped high mount cab over engine type. Pressure is mounting to revise length limitations to provide increased driver comfort, better ride, and greater safety.
- Diesel engines dominate the heavy truck field with penetration in the over 33,000 pounds gross vehicle weight rating class up to 95%. Diesel engine usage is also increasing substantially in the 26,001-33,000 pounds class, and just beginning to increase in the 19,501-26,000 pounds class.
- While diesel engines up to 600 horsepower are available for truck use, engines in the 270-350 horsepower range are normally used in over the road tractors. There is a substantial increase in turbo-charging and after-cooling to reduce emissions and engine noise; slower engine speeds (as low as 1800 r.p.m.) are being provided to reduce noise and improve fuel economy.
- Diesel engine emissions subject to increasing severity.
- Additional Federal Safety Standards including the controversial standard No. 121, Air Brake Systems, which mandated the use of an anti-lock system on the basis of its performance requirements, became effective. Courts subsequently ruled out the anti-lock systems.

- Federal exterior noise control limits applicable to trucks as manufactured became effective January 1, 1978; increasingly severe requirements effective January 1, 1982.
- Cab interior noise limits applicable to trucks in operation established by the Bureau of Motor Carrier Safety.
- Manufacturers of heavy trucks developed a voluntary fuel economy improvement program which has saved over 3.9 billion gallons of fuel since 1973. Many manufacturers have made available fuel savings packages consisting of fuel efficient diesel engines, demand actuated fans, radial tires, aerodynamic drag-reducing devices, axle ratios, and engine speeds tailored for the 55 m.p.h. speed limit, and transmission ratios designed to keep the engine operating in its most effective speed range.
- Front axles with aluminum beams introduced and used in small quantities.
- Automatic slack adjusters for brakes made available.
- Air actuated disc brakes made available by several manufacturers.

Typical of the trucks produced in the 1971-80 time period are the following:

2 Axle Short Conventional Tractor — This tractor (Figure 33) is of the short nose conventional design with a 90" dimension from bumper to back of cab. This particular tractor hauls a 45 foot semi-trailer within 55 foot overall length. The front bumper has been 'bobbed' by cutting off the outer ends to prevent them from being forced back against the front tires in case of an accident, possibly causing the driver to lose control of the vehicle.

3 Axle Refuse Truck — The illustration (Figure 34) shows a construction type 3 axle truck of conventional design with a set-back front axle and heavy frame rails set up for use with a large compacting type refuse body. As population increases and land fills become further apart, there will be an ever-increasing need for more trucks to handle refuse and garbage.

3 Axle Cab Over Engine Tractor with Normal Width

Figure 33
White Road Boss Conventional Tractor (1972) (Photograph furnished through the courtesy of the White Motor Corporation)

Figure 34
White Heavy-Duty Refuse Truck (1973) (Photograph furnished through the courtesy of the White Motor Corporation)

Sleeper Berth — Typical of tractors intended for owner-operators is the White Road Commander 2 cab over engine model equipped with a normal width sleeper berth and which features custom painting and many chrome plated and polished aluminum items. While fleets normally specify engines in the 270-320 horsepower range to haul 80,000 pounds gross combination weight, owner-operators often specify 350-450 horsepower engines to increase average operating speeds.

Mack F Series Cab Over Engine Tractor — Introduced in 1962, the Mack F series cab over engine tractors continue in production, and are available with either non-sleeper or sleeper cabs of the forward tilting type. The cab is fitted with a large two piece curved glass windshield to assist in reducing both air resistance and the amount of splash and spray thrown on the door windows and mirrors.

Offset Cab Installation — The Mack U series short nose conventional tractor features an offset cab installation, primarily to provide increased foot room between the left side of the cab and the engine housing projecting into the cab.

Mack Construction Type Trucks — These Mack DM series construction trucks are produced in a relatively wide range of capacities. The cab is offset to the left on this series. Some of the models in this series can be equipped with a steel butterfly type hood and with heavy pit type fenders, or with an integral forward tilting reinforced fiberglass hood and fender assembly.

SAE Fuel Economy Test Program — As a part of the Voluntary Fuel Economy Improvement Program, a number of truck manufacturers provided pairs of trucks of varying configurations and gross weights for test purposes to verify the SAE Fuel Economy Prediction Procedure and to determine the improvements in fuel economy obtained in several fleet operations. Each pair included a 'standard' truck and a 'fuel efficient' truck. The trucks illustrated (Figure 35) were of identical specifications except that the

Figure 35
SAE Fuel Economy Test Trucks (1979) (Photograph furnished through the courtesy of the White Motor Corporation)

fuel efficient truck was equipped with a fuel savings package of the type previously described. Fuel savings in excess of 25% have been obtained in operating these trucks in fleet operations.

The foregoing briefly summarized the progress which has been made in the development of motor trucks over a period of approximately 80 years. What about the future? What can we look for in the way of future motor truck developments?

A factor that has become of increasing importance during the past ten years is the role of government legislation, standards, and regulations in the design of motor trucks. Among such items are the following:

- Federal and state motor vehicle size and weight limits.
- Federal motor vehicle safety standards.
- Federal and California emissions standards.
- Revisions in and additions to Federal Motor Carrier Safety Regulations.
- Federal and state noise limitations: (a) Exterior, (b) Cab Interior.
- State equipment requirements.

Much of the work of engineering departments involved in the design of trucks and components for such heavy trucks has in recent years been devoted to ensuring conformance with applicable legislation, standards, and regulations by such vehicles and combinations. There will be a continuing trend toward more severe restrictions with the result that substantial amounts of engineering effort will continue to be devoted to meeting these more severe limitations.

One of the subjects of considerable interest in connection with future trucks is the type of power plant to be used. In recent years, heavy trucks have largely been diesel powered with an increasing trend toward turbo-charged and to turbo-charged and after-cooled engines. Medium duty trucks are now rapidly becoming diesel powered, while diesel engine penetration in trucks in the gross vehicle weight range of 19,501-26,000 pounds is increasing, but at a more moderate pace.

It is anticipated that the trend toward more diesel engines will continue, with at least 50% of the 19,501-26,000 pounds G.V.W. range being diesel powered by the late 1980s.

However, consideration has been given to alternate types of power plants such as the Stirling external combustion engine, the stratified charge gasoline engine, and the gas turbine. In addition, advanced development work is being done on diesel engines to provide turbo-compound engines and 'insulated' engines.

The turbo-compound engine uses exhaust gas to operate a power producing expansion turbine connected to the engine output shaft in addition to providing a turbocharger to force more air into the engine and increase its output.

The 'insulated' engine is one in which the cooling system is replaced with high temperature resistant materials in the combustion and cylinder areas to capture more of the heat energy in the form of engine output. Both of these types of engines will provide increased efficiency and lower heat losses than the present turbo-charged and aftercooled engines and appear to be realistic extensions of diesel engine development.

At the present time, relatively little development work is being done on Stirling and stratified charged gasoline engines for heavy trucks because of high development costs. While the Stirling engine provides advantages with respect to possible multi-fuel use, good fuel economy, and high thermal efficiency, it is expected to be expensive to manufacture and require substantial development cost.

The gas turbine was of substantial interest during the late 1950s. A number of manufacturers developed turbines and installed them in trucks. Generally, it was found that the fuel economy of the gas turbine was inferior to that of the diesel engine, particularly at partial load. In addition, significantly higher initial costs were involved. Advantages of the gas turbine included easier start-up and less vibration, but as a result of the inferior fuel economy, there has been less interest in the use of gas turbines for heavy trucks.

Any alternative power plant must be able to match the life cycle cost of not only current diesel engines but diesel engines that may be developed in the near future. In addition to life cycle cost, factors that must be evaluated in comparing power plants include the following:
- Fuel consumption
- Emissions
- Noise
- Reliability and durability
- Application (suitability for truck use)
- Cost effectiveness
- Availability of accessory drives
- Performance

The diesel engine in many areas is a moving target. For example, continued improvements in fuel economy have reduced brake specific fuel consumption to 0.35 pounds per brake horsepower-hour, whereas several years ago, specific consumption factors of 0.4 to 0.45 were not uncommon.

Another factor that precludes the volume use of alternate power plants in truck service for many years is the time cycle required to prove out and build up the acceptance of an alternate power plant. In the case of diesel engines, the first diesel engines were installed in trucks in the U. S. in 1931, but it was not until the late 1950s that diesels really came into their own on heavy trucks.

What else can we expect with respect to future truck designs? Some of the important changes are the following:
- Greater emphasis on trucks of conventional design as overall lengths increase and become more uniform.
- Improved driver environment including lower noise levels; lower maximum interior temperatures; reduced fumes; greater interior space and dimensions; improved

seating; better heating, ventilating, and air conditioning systems; and improved defroster and demisting systems.
- Improved truck ride including better balanced tires and wheel assemblies; stiffer truck frames; suspended cabs and seats; improved suspensions; and better dimensional relationships such as the location of the front axle.
- Improved fuel efficiency by means of better combustion; aerodynamic designs (less air resistance); radial tires; more use of turbo-charged and aftercooled diesel engines and computer selected drive line components and ratios tailored for the specific operation.
- Increased usage of gear driven engine accessories.
- Electronic digital instrument readouts and diagnostic systems.
- Improved reliability and durability (the 500,000 mile truck with limited maintenance and with no major overhauls).
- Increasing use of lightweight and high strength materials including graphite-fiber-reinforced plastics, other plastics, and lightweight aluminum and magnesium alloys.

Based on past history and current trends, it is anticipated that future truck developments will be evolutionary in nature, and not revolutionary. We must not lose sight of the fact that a truck is a work unit and must operate efficiently and economically with a minimum of downtime. For this reason alone, relatively radical new designs will have to prove to be acceptable and economical over the normal extended life of a truck before gaining any appreciable acceptance.